ANKLE-DEEP IN PACIFIC WATER

Ankle-Deep in Pacific Water

Poems

E. Hughes

Haymarket Books
Chicago, Illinois

© 2024 Erica Hughes

Published in 2024 by
Haymarket Books
P.O. Box 180165
Chicago, IL 60618
773-583-7884
www.haymarketbooks.org
info@haymarketbooks.org

ISBN: 979-8-88890-260-8

Distributed to the trade in the US through Consortium Book Sales and Distri-
bution (www.cbsd.com) and internationally through Ingram Publisher Services
International (www.ingramcontent.com).

This book was published with the generous support of Lannan Foundation,
Marguerite Casey Foundation, and Wallace Action Fund.

Special discounts are available for bulk purchases by organizations and institu-
tions. Please email info@haymarketbooks.org for more information.

Cover photograph of *I Wanted to Give You the Ocean* © 2019 by Nastassja E.
Swift. Sculpture: wool, cotton, wire, metal, concrete, seaweed, sand, ocean water,
48 x 28 x 24 inches.

Cover design by Rachel Cohen.

Library of Congress Cataloging-in-Publication data is available.

10 9 8 7 6 5 4 3 2 1

for my mother

History [is] an open wound . . .
—SAIDIYA HARTMAN

CONTENTS

3

Black Women Standing Ankle-Deep in Pacific Water

c. African American Museum and Library, Oakland 2019

The likeness of four women is rendered mono-
chrome on a white banner—the floral

patterns on their cotton dresses and their straw
sunhats, ornamented in satin ribbons,

are obscured by shutter and light. Their long sleeves
gather loosely at the elbow giving time away—

perhaps the photo was taken in the 1920s or 30s
—some forty years before my grandparents became

migrants. The women stand ankle-deep in Pacific
water, perhaps on an eastern shore

of the San Francisco Bay, hands pressed
to their caps, careful not to let the diablos

winds catch their hats, careful not to allow
a determined sun on their brown faces.

It looks as if it were a clear day—perfect
to capture this moment: a hill slowly

ascending and waning, the sagebrush grasped
in wind blowing gracefully toward tightly

packed sand, saltwater rippling gently against
the petite banks of the women's ankles.

Each's happiness seems simple—a warm day
by water miles from Jim Crow and history.

Now as I stand, my neck craned for my need,
looking toward this past, I want

these women to tell me something new of survival—
of the cruel way light obscures pain. In this photo,

I see mostly my dispossession—the buried story
of the West's fathomless past—ordinary, opaque

with all of it rupturing.

1

I Ran Until I Could No Longer

catch wafts of ocean salt or hot tar
in the air, crossing over miles of rural
terrain until there was no evidence
of home, just the backbone of the Sierras
and everything I have failed to put
to language. I have avoided the details
of terror: the cockroaches crawling
up my legs while I slept at a friend's
house, how they laid eggs in the walls,
my third-grade teacher who called
the cops on me as I sat in a field crying
about a bully, the floors I slept on,
the empty refrigerators, how
ringworm grew mauve on my cousin's
right thigh, the boy who begged me
to show him my undeveloped *chee-chees*
and took polaroid pictures of them
that developed too quickly in summer
light, the way my mother beat me for it.
In the present, no one believes me
when I say *We rarely saw the ocean* or
It's the children who are the silent causalities
of unprotection or *Even now, the memories*
siphon through me instead of blood.

After a Beating

I offered my mother the cracked alabaster jar
    of my child body, trying to heal the wreckage of us.

She sat beneath the window, on our black loveseat,
    in our one-bedroom apartment—her left hand

curled like a branch under her chin. I approached,
    laid my forehead against her shoulder. As if to say—

I didn't mean it, Mommy.
    She stiffened and lifted my eager head from her body.

Now, she said, they'll take you away from me.
    I sat in the empty seat beside her, watching the light

of the afternoon spill through the blinds, refracting off
    white walls, striping my mother's honey-brown face blue.

my mother wakes at night
    to clean the dishes. The dog
on his back snores as she passes
    through the living room
like a ghost in a floral night-
    gown. She's always been
the elusive love in my life—
    expansive as memory
over a battered body. The moon
    dignified in the sky peers
through the kitchen window
    with the will of all its light. Light
traipses through water and water
    envelops my mother's hands.
How her hands have torqued
    my dark body—a kind of light
I have never understood illuminating
    the past: Here are my mother's
hands scrubbing my dirty dishes.
    Here are my mother's hands
clutching a belt like a horse breaker.
    Here are her hands holding
the larynx of a broom, punishing
    my body like god. My God,
who loves me and clutches me
    by the throat, says—*I'll beat you*
like a bitch off the street.

Portrait of My Father

c. Oakland, 1999

He sat quietly in a chair, one leg crossed over the other
along the lap of the burgundy seat, a glass of Hennessey

tilted in one hand, and cigarette burning down to its filter
in the other. He watched my brother and I spin dimes on

the nightstand. He laughed a little, perhaps at our innocence—
the way children can make a game out of nothing—as we

crafted a competition with loose change from his pockets.
That night, I watched moonlight drip into our room—glow

bowing around the rusting bars scoring our only window.
My brother slept securely between us, his mouth open, fat

cheek pushed against a flat pillow. When a woman on
the street screamed, I woke in the purgatory of predawn

and night to see my father throw his share of the covers
on my brother, and curl his back into a crescent moon before

reaching for a Marlboro Red and striking his thumb against
the metal wheel of a lighter. He balanced the roll of tobacco

between his lips and tilted his head as he weaved a nest with
his fingers, guiding the tiny, blue flame toward the end

of the shaft. Smoke rising like prayer, I watched my father
who, for the first time, was not the shadow that stalked

my mother, or the shadow that hated how much I reminded
him of her. For the first time, my father seemed like a man

broken in the same way light fractures at dawn

TRIPTYCH

they have both marked me / with their blind and terrible love
—AUDRE LORDE

I.

My father is the dark shadow—obscured
      by the mark of someone's careless
fingertip on the lens. He embraces me—

my face somewhere in the ache of his
      pointed shoulder. Seeing the picture now,
I know he grins with the power to make me his

obedient daughter, though I am uncomfortable
      there in his lap—my body limp, as heavy
as a child can make her body heavy.

It must be my grandmother's birthday party.
      She shuffles away from the frame wearing
a crown—red, white, and gold. My father

in the foreground. I can feel his warm breath
      in my ear—*Don't you love me? Don't you love
your daddy?*—tobacco and alcohol fixed in his smell.

We sit on my grandmother's striped black and gold
      couch. Above us, pictures of black figures
in bright colors dance seemingly off the wall.

2.

Even after my father   threw a brick through
      my and my sister's   window—
after the broken   glass on the carpet became
      a montage of refraction   and stars. Someone
thought to take this picture: my father a skeleton,
      a shadow man.   Darkness no longer matters.
Bound by light and time, I am trying to   escape
      into the foreground of the picture, pushing
   away   from his bird chest   as he smiles,
            but he is holding me still
as if I owe him something   of myself. He demands
      my love, and I want nothing more
            than to escape the violence
      of his voice.   The danger of his psyche.
         According to my mother,   he saved my life
                  because he married her—so she would not
                        end the pregnancy.

3.

My grandmother died in spring. I collect photos
I haven't seen in years from her mobile home.
I show my mother this picture: I must be five

or six front teeth missing, twists coming undone
in ponytail after having lost a barrette. I think this
frame of my life then is playful, funny even—

something of the past we could agree on. She says,
I had nothing to do with you—your hair or your name.
That was your Daddy and Nana. I look down at this

picture. On the back, I have managed to spell my own
name—E R I C A—knowing it would be many years
before I would learn that the mournful sound of letters

together make meaning. She continues, *Erica Tiffany—*
E.T.—I was afraid the kids would think you were an alien.
My mother tells me this almost as confession, laughing,

twenty-eight years after giving birth. She refuses
to say what she regrets—the life, the shame, the foreign
body—the sound *I should have aborted you* makes.

Rupture in Memory

—*after Louis Glück's poem "Faithful and Virtuous Night"*

My story began in pieces—in the wake of four migrations,
in my mother's and father's initial exchange, in the heat
of confinement and emancipation. I began like a whip
of lightning in a night sky, a moment shared between two

hurting people. If it is difficult to recover from the body,
fathom what it is to endure.   In autumn, the wind-
chimes mused. The bluebird and the woodpecker chirped
trepidly. Constituent, the memoirs of our large memory.

Points of terror in a heat shimmer of the mind sporadically
understood like a mountain posed for a black child to overcome.
Mountain where can you take us? Behind me, It says, *the desert.*
Not—*I am the way to understanding the source of your pain.*   Imagine,

the painted yellow stars against blue sky on my bedroom
wall conveying an atmosphere of loss, impressions of beatings
in the form of dreams, stars as one cast into an ocean.
I shared this atmospheric room with my brother.

To punish him for not being beaten by our mother, I kept him
awake at night, kicking the bottom of his mattress until my fear
of the dark gave me to the hands of exhaustion. The habits
of childhood: My brother on his back singing, envisioning

the elusive future until he falls asleep. At the time, my brother
sang more than he spoke, and he sang a song he called "There Can be
Miracles." Did he sing that song the first night we were the only ones
in our family to share a room? *No*—it was a night

during childhood. A summer bird carried hope like a jewel
in its beak, then flew away from me. Like the soft arias of birds,

agony arose and fell in my mind as often as breath in my lungs.
While listening to my brother, I lay on the bottom bunk

staring at the metal bars above me. *Run away from here.* I would
think. It reminded me of what I could not escape—my mother's
rage but more painfully the stories about how she never loved
my father, whom I hated, too. In this case, the thin veil

between generations torn and each woman left with her own
piercing memories.   Picture, if you will, an autumn day further
back in my past—I rode my bike, above me storm clouds in the sky.
In one hand, the wrist of my favorite doll. In the other,

the handlebar. On my back, everything I needed to endure
the circled route of the apartment parking lot. My sister found me
mid-journey stowed away in the laundromat moaning *I want
to disappear.*

She sat me on a machine and laughed the way older people do
at the pain of children. She said *Boo Boo, tell me what happened*—
then I disappeared. Perhaps this is the inherited work of a child—
to retreat and endure.   Picture another scene in autumn,

each family member laboring privately over our memories.
The piano resonated as my grandmother's hands trembled
over the keys. From her song—*A healing stream flows from
Calvary's mountain.* Then my mother's voice buckled—

Till my ransomed soul shall find rest beyond the river—. Wistful,
are you wistful? Do you want to return to those moments
around the piano with your family? For the piano's song
to break against the indigo night of your suffering, offering

you the solace of your mother's voice? This, of course, will
offer you no relief. Still, here is my brother, grandmother,

and mother singing and striking against the prison of my mind.
Mid to late October, another memory: The sky was clear

as any day in California, ajar as the books I used to build
dollhouses with. In this book, a pink pig sits on a chair, says
something to the reader. I will not be able to read until I am
twenty-one. On page four, I rub my fingers across the pastel

picture of a green frog. On the last page, the frog and
the pig unite in an embrace. It is still too many years before
I understand progression or story. Underneath me, black hands
pull me toward an ending. Whose hands could they be?

Anyone's from any time—.

Even Now

My mother spent hours making   sure
     my ponytails were perfect   that I had
the knockers to   match my outfits,   saved money
     shopping at the canned-food store   for green beans
and corn, spent forty hours   a week working
     with white men who would call her
outside of her name   —Bitch!
     She provided the roof   (no matter
how minor or how imperfect   it was) over our heads.
     She tells me this now to prove she did her best
at mothering—as if to redress the ways she made
     my insignificant life   then fathomless.
Even now,   she doesn't address the beatings—
     the way she would   swing the belt   like a woman
with nothing to lose.   Somehow, I want to   forget
     the way her hands snatched me
from a chair and swung   at my child body
     like I were a grown man—
the memory of my sister peeling   our mother off of me,
     begging, *Mommy! Please! Stop!*—   the memory
of the way I loved my mother,   would offer
     the weight of myself   at the altar of her chest
when she was too tired to push me away.
     Even now, she says—   It was the depression
that made me so angry,   so unforgiving—
     but I've learned my lesson because   god
shattered a glass table   when I screamed at him
     —*Take my life.*

Mother,

      strange is the lineage of our pain—   its smallness,
the rivers of its past,   passed like milk

      between mothers and their daughters.
Even now,

      I don't say *Mom*—   you lost your will to live,
and I begged god to kill me too,

      begged god to   take me from this
violet arrangement   of suffering.

      I asked him for your hands   to be wrapped
like a gentle lead   around me, begged your

      hands be the ones   to murder me.

Neglect or Baptism Listicle

I.

Once my foot

turned blue

\

and you

complained

about taking

me to the hospital—.

I forced myself

to walk

when I couldn't—

that ankle now   blessed

arthritic.

2.

I rarely complained

I couldn't see   until I was

seventeen—   the stigma-

tism in my left eye straining

to see the world—until I begged,

begged to see

the optometrist.

3.

When I stepped outside for the first time

I gasped—*Look,*

how green the trees.

17

4.

    The wisdom

                    teeth that grew

          in the ground of my gums

              when I was fifteen

began crowding

           my perfect smile—

    that wisdom

           went unattended, is now rotten

unpulled and capped silver

                  in the back of my mouth.

    My new crooked   smile is tested

        by the passion of that

unlove.

5.

The keloids   on my top and

      lower lips   mark times I needed

stitches—the old

      wounds were desperate

for any shape

      of healing—my body

            made new

      in the blue flame

           of your disregard.

I Called Home in January

c. Siskiyou County, 2011

When she answered, I managed—Mom—
noticed the way the alpine trees stood
like hair on the white peaks of Mount Shasta

and a single mockingbird calling instinctively
from a tree into green silence. I called into
my own tender darkness holding my mother's

breath to my ear—memory spun like a gyre
in my stomach: She told me once I was her
heaviest child at eight pounds, the weight that

positioned itself posterior and collapsed her
pelvic bone. She watched me splatter myself
from her insides and into existence in a ceiling

mirror. What a horrific sight it all must have been—
tolerating some grey growth's violence then
its expectation to be loved. I rummaged for light

leafing its way through thick forest and I fought
an urge to jump from the nearest cliff asking god
if he had looked into the mirror as she gave me life,

if he had tolerated the same reflection she had—
my swollen face, my half-unborn body twisting
out between her thighs.

BECKWOURTH PASS

c. SIERRA NEVADA, 2015

The oak, redwood, and laurel alike were dying
or dead—ochre and combustible as matches.
My father was not as thin as I had remembered.
His belly protruded over the band of the seatbelt
as I tried to remember what the trees were like
before they caught drought—deeply green and
heavy with pines and life? Maybe. How easily I had
forgotten what I grew up seeing—even at a distance.
Words were difficult to find as he drove the car,
sputtering at an incline. He had not wanted me
to drive almost 1,800 miles alone over an unforgiving
mountain, through a salt desert and midwestern
prairie—now greener than the Sierra Nevada's
expanse of trees. He wanted me to find
someone else to take his place on the journey,
to pack their bags in with the last of my belongings.
That stuff is too heavy for this little car to tow, to carry
such a far distance, he said. My father has driven
more than one woman he loves over this mountain:
First, my mother when they eloped—I was only
a shadow in my mother's womb heavy with
an unbearable decision—*To break me or to let me live?*
My father's eyes were on the road when he asked
if I remembered the time he took my brother
and me sledding. *Remember how slick the ice was?*
How steep the slope? He grinned. I refused a response
as if to say—*I remember nothing.* Yet, someone else's

blood staining packed ice entered my mind. The crack
of skull on frozen ground, and my father's hand
leading me up the slopes regardless. When we arrived
in Reno, we stopped at a diner; he ate more
than I had ever seen him consume—a sign of sobriety.
Again, he said, *Remember when you were little? How we used
to feed the ducks bits of bread? We had fun. Didn't we always
have fun?* When he asked this, he seemed stuck in time,
nauseated by the demands of the past. Lifting his head
from the plate, he asked, *I was a good father to you? Right?*

As Her Feet Tap the Brass Pedals

c. Madera, 2016

I recognize my mother—   her mouth
      once framed   a gapped-
         tooth smile. Now,
it is eroded   by periodontitis
           where implants
    stand perfectly white
         drilled into the old
   sockets of her jawbone.
         Her fingers manage
   melody without score.
          In music,
my mother can't scare
     me—the dark circles
        perched
          like birds beneath
   her eyes
      now something I see
    in my own
      reflection.
At the breast
    of the piano, she sings
  —*Memories*

        light the corners of my mind
and I cross   the chasm
       between mother
         and daughter
   as if to say, *Please*—

stop playing this wounding

part of the song.

—Because of *The Way We Were*

What Should We Call This Space

between us—its dark outlines given
to the bleak pressures of subtly now
after *this* many years? There was never
a goodbye. I don't remember if I packed
my bags or if you found your last bit
of motherly strength to help me clear
my things from our home. I remember
only that day in slow impressions: the old,
turquoise truck—the slowest vehicle
on the road—heavy with luggage and
a twin mattress swaying in parched winds.
The sun at its lowest point right before
sunset broke violet over our faces.
It smelled like heat, petrol, and orange
blossoms. I don't remember when we
arrived or the part where we unpacked,
perhaps in silence. I don't remember
if you kissed me before pulling away—
the leaving was *that* destructive,
an invisible line drawn in time between
what we were and what can't be now.

APORIA

I have made a small world of this loss—
    my mother's hand raising—not to strike—
but to smooth the edges of my hair
    with a toothbrush. The pyrite and bones

uncovered in the yard, the walls scarred
    by the force of my body, the memories
hooking down the chest of my mind. Grief
    is a culture, a collection of fragments,

firmament of matter, manner by which I
    become a mosaic of my losses.
None of this will make sense until I look back,
    see how the sharp edges have, somehow,

come together. I hold my brother's and sister's
    hands through this exhibition, say *This is*
where I hurt you—I am sorry. There are pictures here
    of our child bodies, almost destroyed

in the crossfires of our mother's private pain,
    in the wake of her private desperation.
Our history refuses to forgive—even as I open
    myself wide enough to hold two truths:

Love and pain.

2

…we know this…to be the ground on which we stand.
—CHRISTINA SHARPE

Any of the old pioneer colored people, when asked concerning her, immediately begin to tell all sorts of queer stories about Mary Ellen ["Mammy"] Pleasant and usually end by saying: "She always wore a poke bonnet and a plaid shawl," and "She was very black, with thin lips." Then sometimes they will also add: She handled more money during the pioneer days in California than any colored person.
—DELILAH L. BEASLEY, FROM *THE NEGRO TRAILBLAZERS OF CALIFORNIA*

The Accounts of Mammy Pleasant

c. San Francisco, 1904

I. TRUTH AND LIES

Call me a great financer, a witch, Queen
Esther—whatever you need to justify
my longstanding status as a free woman
and why I was the one who possessed all
that money. It does not matter how
I got here—I am. Despite all those years
I spent fighting, there is nothing new
I can tell you of the horrors of captivity.
Yet I can tell you of my husband's kind-
hearted eyes and the hook scar
just above his lip, and how I threw myself
into the service of the underground after
his death. You see, south of the Canadian
line, freedom slips the imagination and
the circadian rhythm of justice is interrupted.
For the slave, there is no such a thing as leisure
—only the constant intrusion, only the bleak
memoirs of loss and confinement. There is
no more time or respect or patience left
in me for white people who own slaves,
nor those who think the plight of
the Negro is himself. Friends make up all
kinds of myths about me. They say, *Mammy*
Pleasant, is it true? You knew John Brown and
handed him all that money for Harpers Ferry?
I say it doesn't matter if it were true (though

it is) but like the night sky, I have tried to hold
two truths. I know the path to freedom is
mysterious—mysterious as losing your
mother's face in memory. Hoodoo or not,
I did whatever it took to steal my people home.

2. MR. PRICE

I had never seen that white man before. He wore

a black coat over his shoulder, shouted—*Girl,*

point me toward town center. I knew town was just East

behind the plantation where I would walk the border

of master's land with my mother after sermon

on Sundays. We would pick mulberries to feed

each other—juice reddening our lips and fingertips.

I was steady working—tried not to mess my picking

rhythm or to look directly in his eyes. I lifted

my finger in the direction of sunrise—said *Yessir,*

town is back behind the clearing. Peace be with you.

Days afterward, the white man returned with freedom

papers, said *I paid good money to save a bright girl like yourself*

and your cleverness from that kind of labor.

I could not save my mother from that kind of labor.
On the morning I left for Nantucket, she hugged me,
kissed my lips, made sure I knew to cross my ankles
when I sat down on the train. She said *Mary Ellen*
do good and listen to everything those white folks say.
She tucked in my hand a single piece of fruit—
the last gift she would ever give me. My papers
were so new then the only creases on the leaves
were made by my former master's seal. How could I
have known the sable image of my mother's face
would fade as quickly as my world would expand?
On the train—home somewhere behind me now—
I took the juice from the mulberry with my thumb,
pressed it to the page—spoke my mother's name.

In Nantucket, the white folks were the same
as they were in Georgia—they just had new
language for drudgery yet were unencumbered

by the fear of a Negro learning to read.
My mistress was ambivalent toward
my learning—as long as I kept up with

the laundry (though my feet and hands soured
in the soap and starch), cooked the fish and beans
they loved to eat, and moved invisibly

about the house. I missed my mother most
in winter, held the memory of her face,
my own reflection, tenderly in my hands

in the warmth of water when I washed.
As I began to learn the alphabet,
mistress whipped me each time I sounded out

Ape-ple instead of *apple* or wrote *whether*
when I meant *Weather—the snow is falling*
outside our window. She called me invalid

and unable to apprehend language
or original thought. I thought and thought
of those moments when my mother rubbed

pig fat in my hair during leisure to keep

the ticks away, so the edges wouldn't break—
as she recounted the rules of root work:

Sorghum is good for when your feet swell up.
Salt your door for protection. Say this prayer—
Keep us, Lord, from sinkin' down—when cleaning

wounds. I have cleaned so many wounds—
except my own. I spent days then washing
the walls, floors, bonnets, undergarments—

determined to learn a new episteme.
I spoke to myself—*Do not give this world*
your flesh. Make callous the feeling of her

lash, of her criticism—learn the curvature,
the ascent and descent of sound with each
stroke of a letter—learn to write your name.

To survive up North, there is no room to groan
about the past. At market in Boston, I thought
about the sable hands who picked the corn, those
beans, hands soaked in water to earn that rice,
that salt. Some dropped dead collecting the sugar
and dried the tobacco the man who called me Gal
smoked in his pipe. It's amazing how little my life
changed in freedom. Slavery refused to wash down
the river of my need—just because someone
scratched what I thought was my name and some
odd phrases down on paper—*Its traces are everywhere.*
I learned this in a new way, a mosaic of suffering,
new scars forming at the base of my back by
the force of Mistress' lash. I grappled with this
quandary for a long while, looking toward the green
terrain of Massachusetts—*How does ground or a body
of water mark freedom or chains? What does it mean to
love when you burden unspeakable pain?* The earth
remembers everything the mind and history cannot
tolerate. At market, the man, who would become
my husband, approached asked if this was my first
time in the city. I nodded, *Yes,* eager to learn about
the music of his Spanish accent. I mentioned Georgia
but not freedom. He smiled, said *I'm Alex: I am here
from Cuba doing God's marvelous work.* Back then,
I could not have known what love was to make of us
or how our bellies were fated to be bloated with loss.
Somehow, my life became tributary flowing into
the force of his life, at the most swollen point of
my need to be known in unspeakable shame.

6. BOIS CAÏMAN

By the sacrificial blood of the black pig,
with the guidance of the loa, the slaves
planned for freedom by the strength of Vodun.

In the fury of the Black Madonna, Ezili Danotor,
they wrote the pact for revolution in indigo—
it was no longer the blood of the Black

that would be spilled. The god Ogún drank his rum
and smoked his pipe in the shadows of the forest
as they danced for freedom by the strength of Vodun.

Ogún raised his machete—declared Ase!—
in the voice and bodies of the people speaking
through the sacrificial blood of the black pig.

And then rose Toussaint Louverture—an imperfect
sun dawning over an island of burning plantations—
leading the war for freedom by the strength

of the stolen. Out of iron chains, spirits lead
the people through eight years of fire and slaughter.
By the sacrificial blood of the black pig,
freedom erupted from the ground—the strength of Vodun.

I scarcely understood how painful
our beauty in that moment, the darkness
of our bodies together, taking refuge
in each other and in the myth of the black
pig, despite the frozen world of the north.
Our bedroom lit by a sole flame.

Tonight, Alex said, *I will tell you of flame*
spirits and death—war a necessary yet painful
journey. The spirits did not guide them north
by stars but in the strength of their own darkness—
vodun. I thought of Gregoria nights, black
as the spread of my mother's hair, a wide refuge

of rest. His left hand climbed the black refuge
of my back. The story he spoke roused a flame
of blue rage and nerve in my chest. *The black*
Madonna, Ezili Danotor, garnered the painful
fury necessary for a slave rebellion. In darkness,
my father would carry the story to me—fleeing north

again from Saint-Domingue to Cuba in his memory. North,
a myth tossed around by the eager for refuge,
I thought, as I surveyed our bedroom in darkness.
Alex's eyes reflected the only light, the flame
of the fire. He held me tighter as if it were too painful
to recall his father's voice. The memory black

as soot on his mind, it seemed. I knew the black
spine of loss when I left my mother for the North.
I knew all a person loses in freedom, a painful
expanse of ache, wide as water, in exchange for refuge,
and I knew all a person gains in the blue flame
of manumission. All of its subtleties, I knew darkness

as I took my time with him, rubbed the darkest
parts of his flesh with balm black
oil. What more could one ask of us? My flame
for revolution began in the misery of the North
as Alex chanted the story of African deities, the refuge
for the captives: *The spirits were pained*—

flame, black, darkness.

8. GOLD RUSH

I'd heard in California anyone could get rich
quick from discovering gold or leasing money
to the miners—and the visage of the Pacific
Ocean bears a deeper color than the Atlantic,
marking the end of the new world. After Alex
died, I thought I would end if I could not see
myself in its waters, so I took what mattered
into my own hands—the bond for his father's
land in Cuba, the notes we passed in love and
his charge—*pursue freedom*. I braved a ship that
began in the Atlantic and sailed through the Gulf
of Mexico. I walked through Panama without
saying a word to my fellow travelers. I braved
another ship sailing to San Francisco hoping
to refuse an arc toward ache, to make loss mean
something other than the blemish of tragedy
it had spread across the sheet of my life. All I knew
to do was run from everything that reminded me
of the way his stern cheek would rest against
my breastbone. In San Francisco, I gave the money
from the sale of his father's land to whatever
poor white soul needed it for a meal, a new
rocker, or pickaxe—as long as it came back
somehow different, more abundant. In my grief,
I amassed a fortune and was changed.

9. ON HARPERS FERRY:
A JOURNEY TO MEET WITH JOHN BROWN

In the bright eye of summer, I carried
the promise I had made my dead
husband as a pendant around my neck
almost 2,500 miles into the freedom
terrain of Canada. In Windsor, I knew
there was only one investment
that could be made toward the final
push for freedom in the United States.
I was one of John's secret donors,
knew nothing was to be gained if one
was unwilling to spend or to take up
arms. On the way, a man told me
John had stunning ocean-blue eyes,
and I thought about the Pacific. Once,
the Portuguese explorer, Ferdinand
Magellan, stood at the edge of the New
World and called this new sea *peaceful*.
Even in San Francisco, a Negro could be
dragged back south in chains. Once,
I saw a fugitive woman be torn from her
husband then loaded onto a clipper
that disappeared into the jowls of the Pacific.
By then, I understood what happens
to the Negro in water, had grown so tired
of the disappearing. I could no longer
care if my life was the ransom for rebellion
against chains. In California, I stood facing
the cold visage of this other ocean, terrified
by who lurks in its waters, knowing what
we were never to become without war.

10. REVOLUTION

In Windsor, I gave John 30,000 dollars and convinced him
we needed more men for the rebellion. I was to go, incite
the enslaved to take up arms with us. I wanted my kind

to know that compliance is no way to live, so I disguised
myself as a jockey, rode a mare as a man and camped
beneath stars, following in reverse the drinking gourd to

West Virginia. I wore no bonnet, my hair tucked into
the black globe of a jockey's hat, slid on my first pair
of trousers, laced my boots up for war. When I crossed

the Mason-Dixon, I was shocked: the news of the raid's
failure and of John's capture was everywhere—*Why
would he go back on our plan? Raid with only twenty-two men?*

I thought. Afterall, it was my mother who birthed me into
the nightmare of a master's arms, life, and labor, my existence
the result of this nation's vile imagination—and I lived in

the hell of that truth every day. I wanted this story to be written
more enigmatic than a white man credited with Negro freedom
or a white man deemed the hero—even in death. I guess this

was my own misstep, my naive hope. Reading the newspapers,
I sank into the pit of myself and imagined what Toussaint
must have felt when he recognized the white light of betrayal—

how the heat of failure settles must have the black crevasses
of his body in the gut of a filthy French prison, dying alone
for trusting they saw him not as a nigger but *human*—

I imagined my name Winnetka—*beautiful*
land—a word I had learned during my travels.
It was a small relief to choose my own name—
signed my initials W.E.P instead of M.E.P,
so no one would suspect my connection to John.
On the train back North to New York, the leaves
were beginning to yellow, the birds in an arrow
knew to fly somewhere warmer, somewhere
less harsh. For the first time in my life, I was
unable to speak, caught in a negotiation with
disappointment and grief—too tired to make
meaning of our rebellion's failure. For the first
time, in a long time, I thought of the plantation
in Georgia, thought of the first time I bled
on cotton—how after so long the callouses made
it seem like the blood in me dried up. I thought
of exhaustion. Lord, there is nothing more profound
than being tired. Near the border, I found shelter
with a group of abolitionists who too were trying
to rework the past, to make loss something more
than sense. By December, they hung John—made
him an argument against war, against freedom. Yet,
what was he to me but an example of the collapse
of love? The dark chasm between the negro and
the white perhaps too long and painful to over-
come. During those nights in hiding, I thought
by candlelight of my mother who died long before
I could buy her to freedom—which some days
I feel is its own myth. *Love is complicated,* many

shout these words at the pain of living—but being
a negro woman with love is a slow death. The small
part of you—the secret parts that are yours and
yours alone—until they aren't—expires with every
loss. No amount of tears will reverse this. *So many
thousands gone*—Isn't that how the song goes?
The blood on the cotton is the only record.

Although he had won the case, been
declared *innocent* of being a fugitive—
I told Archy Lee he could not come back,
to stay and live in Canada if he could.
There, I thought, *he would find some hope.*
I knew he was hardheaded. After all,
he had jumped from a steamboat headed
to San Francisco—refusing to be lead back
to Mississippi by his master, Mr. Stovall.
Archy spent so much of his short life
running, rebuking the chains he was
born into. Yet, he came back, perhaps
looking for home, his people. After
the war, negros all over the country
were looking for their lost, their dead.
Maybe he felt he had vanished, evaporated
like mist in the memory of his beloveds.
Maybe he wanted to be like Lazarus,
the miracle raised from that disappeared
place for his mother. *I heard he was sick.*
Maybe he had not wanted to die without
seeing her again, thought that he could
finally be free in the nation he was born in.
But his master had the longest memory:
When Archy crossed the border south
Mr. Stovall had him arrested, had the case
revived, took it to the Supreme Court—
determined to earn the nigger he lost
back seventeen years after that nigger

was declared free of him and almost
a decade after the conclusion of war.
Stovall lost the case against Archy again—
trying anything to keep that boy in chains.
They found his head first—sticking up
out of sand in a marsh near Sacramento.
They reported he was trying to stave off
the cold, so he buried himself. I say some-
one had decided what would become of
Archy's life: If he refused to be a slave—

        he would be a corpse.

13. DENOUEMENT

In the mansion called the House of Mystery,
they say I killed my own friend Tom Bell—

threw him over the banister like a black
devil, since I was supposedly mentioned

in his will and in a depth of solvency.
They say I was possessed when I did it—

saw the future and Tom refused me that light.
This, of course, was moonshine. Shortly after

his death, I drowned in debt. Wealth and
friends—all gone. What else could I pen

about my life? I was *loved* and *hated*
like everyone who attempts to live beyond

their lots in this dammed life. Once I was
a slave and then I was free, and it wasn't

a miracle. It was full of loss like a man's face
just as he falls beneath the water's opaque

surface. In a dream, I held his face with both
hands and tried not to kiss him. Instead, I let

the outline of his black face and his expression
take me wherever he needed me to go. Freedom

was never spoken—it lived in his look, a silent
moaning in a stranger's face, vibrating

between two unknown persons. Awake,
I carried his face with me on every journey,

even into that courtroom where my wealth
dissolved like sugar on a white man's tongue

and called out to him *Daddy*, I called out to
him *Mama*. I made sure to call him *Baby*.

In San Francisco, the land
    testifies in a long moan
to life's cruelty—sings a blue-
    toned wistfulness, not
the sorrow, the blood and
    mud and the low dirges
my mother hummed like
    grit in her throat,
slaving in a white man's
    fields. So much paradox
on this peninsula—caught
    in the tension between
bay and ocean, freedom
    and unfreedom, irresolute
as the earth's abating tune,
    the syncopation of salt
and wind, those bold colors
    at sunset: fuchsia, gold,
and emerald. Wildfires and
    arctic chills persistent,
even in all this sunshine.
    What I remember of
my loneliness is the wound
    of burdening others
and myself in memory,
    and the brutality of change:
It was as sudden as a cry—
    the way I became free.

3

...if we choose

to keep any part of what is behind us,
we must take all of it
—NATASHA TRETHEWEY

Historiography

c. Redwood City, 1950

The redwoods careen over the Santa Cruz
    Mountains with the compulsion of
stampeding herds. The expanse of pine,
    green as ache, splinters from the ground
like shrines erect for a god full of promises.
    Looking to the mountains and redwoods
as signs for progress and salvation, Big
    Mama followed her sons to this forest
by the bay. Redwood City, a refuge for Black
    folk fleeing the deathly current
of the South. Big Mama ran from Noxapater
    and that house that sat up on bricks
with holes in the subflooring that the rats
    would get through. Big Mama ran
from Big Daddy his violent, drunken stupors
    that colored her life. She left it all south.
California must be better than the North—New York,
    Detroit, and Chicago—she must have said
to herself expecting it to be true, expecting
    the unresolved past stays deadened, unalive
in the need of her grandchildren. Her past is buried
    in a capsule at the base of a cypress tree
that grows in the bay of our heart—in this ledger
    there are the groanings of women, the callous
calls of children eaten by secret and violent fathers
    and mothers, and grandmothers, heart-rhythms

of our family who would say, *None of us suffered*—
  Yet here we are burning in the aftermath.

MEET-CUTE IN REDWOOD CITY

My grandmother tells me there were clubs strung
     like a string of pearls draped along the dark
neck of a woman up and down the peninsula.
     Music and lights at night warbled along the coast
of the bay. She wants to avoid the past and its routine
     burden of memory. The year was 1960:
Myra had just turned eighteen, was fresh up from Texas—
     running from that three-room house, her mama's
church—the heat of her minister preaching fire
     and brimstone—and those opossum carcasses
Daddy Buster would bring in to stew after working
     the crop. I can imagine my grandmother—thin
ankles, a fresh press in her hair, the drawn-out drones
     B. B. King drawing her further and further into
the watering hole where she would meet my grandfather—
     the slick twenty-eight-year-old in a pinstriped suit,
who would part the crowd, take her hand and say—
     Pretty woman, my name's Jimmy.

BAD HABIT

Jimmy came back   from Korea wounded

     in his heart.   He lies on his back

       on his brother's couch   —the popcorn

ceiling somehow   reminds him of the green,

     hilly terrain   he marched with his

         battalion.   In Milpitas,

     he wishes   something else had

become of his life   —perhaps its   ending.

     His nephews run around the living   room

       shooting each other   with their pretend

rifles made by the simple   lift of their child

     thumbs in opposition   of their index fingers.

Shut up—   Jimmy yells *Y'all, go outside now.*   He takes

     another swig of gin   hoping the headache

     would subside.   His wife hit him again

     over the head   with a pan,

       and he somehow managed

to escape—   before she and his eldest

     daughter tied him up.   He had managed

       to drive sixteen miles—despite

all that liquor in him   —to his brother's   place

     before he pissed himself.

     He rubs   the knot radiating   at the back

     of his head. It is too much,

the memory of the gun—   its explosion and precision

     bloody   in the body. It is too much

       the memory   of Big Daddy kidnapping   him.

     It is too much for him   to say   —*Please*

       I am tired of fighting.

like the extension cords. The way my drunk grandfather must have balled his large, calloused hands into a fist and wore the wires like brass knuckles. The way he must have snatched the arm of his eldest daughter, my mother. Twelve years old. The way he must have whipped her good. His janitor overalls probably smelled of gin and sweat and piss. She must have remembered the smell keenly—wet and musky like the bar he frequented; where he would leave her and her siblings in the cold Pontiac in the parking lot for hours until he was finished drowning. She, by now, learned not to cry over her father's beatings—but to take it. Must have learned to tell herself *He doesn't know any better. I must deserve this.* Must have learned to call his touch love. My grandmother, down the hall, does not intervene as he whips her. *Kim!* she must have yelled when he was done—*Have you finished the dishes yet?*

ROUTINE

C. 1971

In a tree, the girl twists wild figs
    from their stems, tilts her head,

remembering Big Mama's lilt—
    Wasps die inside before they bloom.

Her mother calls from the driveway—
    Kimmy! They make their way

from the small home they rent
    in Melo Park to a mansion

near Stanford, singing along
    with the Delfonics on the radio—

Didn't I blow your mind this time?
    Didn't I? The mother stands

in the foyer pointing toward
    the laundry room acknowledging

the dailiness of her being—*someone must*
    feed these kids—as light refracts

diamonds on her skin as if embraced
    in the holiness of a cathedral god.

You clean the stains while I iron the sheets
    and blouses, my grandmother says.

Mother and daughter make this
    a weekly routine, cleaning

the filth of white folks together,
  even here—. I see my mother's

child hands submerged in water.
  The smell of fruit and earth

and the gentleness of girlhood
  washed quietly away.

BARBERSHOP

c. MENLO PARK, 1976

Leonard honks and waves at his sister as she drives
away. He assumes his nieces and nephews are still
asleep because the morning hasn't yet burned off
the fog. He lifts the garage open and notices her
husband hasn't put the sand out over that oil stain
like he asked him to. He pulls the barber chair from
the corner, sets out a pair of clippers, brushes the old
hair out of them and turns on the radio before
the neighborhood greets the morning's song. He stops
on an old-timey record that reminds him of his mama
and daddy and the way his mornings used to begin
with his hands in the earth, pulling up rutabaga and
potatoes. Each Saturday, Leonard makes the trip
from Sunnyvale, from the integrated neighborhood,
from the large house only a chemist's salary can afford,
to Menlo Park. This was the first home he purchased
with the money he earned for surviving war. The youngest
nephew wakes and sits in the corner, watching his uncle
pick out hair and shape with the skill of a master
sculptor—hair like wood shavings falling around his feet.
The boy eats a bowl of cornflakes with water. On the lawn,
the two nieces laugh and talk with their friends about
which boys look the most transformed by their haircuts,
while the eldest boy is off somewhere alone with a girl.
Before the day ends, Leonard buys the children a hot dog,
hands them each a nickel, hoping *somehow* it will be enough.

Meet-Cute in Menlo Park

c. 1975

The fog has just burned off the morning, leaving the day
bright and dry. An eleven-year-old boy in a tie and black
slacks approaches a girl. He holds a shoebox full of rocks.
Do you want to see what I found? he asks. The children from
the neighborhood play cops and robbers around them—
dodging bullets and putting the bad guys in handcuffs
at the shore of the San Francisco Bay. Why do you dress so
funny, like a bishop? the girl asks. She feels a new hole wearing
into the sole of her sock, sneaks a look at her jeans fraying
down the pant leg and the green Chuck Taylors that cover
her shame. My mama always wants her children to look nice, says
the boy. The girl counters, Well you look like you just got out
of church. They both laugh. In this moment between children,
the boy who will become my drunken father must think
of only one thing: the gap still widening between my mother's teeth
as he opens his box to an assortment of wet pillars of earth.
Their story begins much like it ends—with children trying
to understand shame—eager to feel any kind of love.

MY MOTHER AT TWENTY-ONE

Imagine what she must have been—hopeful,
the gap still between her teeth. The reality of

the future still foggy and at bay in the burgundy
of her eyes—some cascading emerald light

at the horizon of herself. She has just become
a mother, still with enough of herself to give

one child. Happiness close enough to touch
like god's brown face during the act prayer.

I imagine it: The apartment the mother and baby
share with their relatives—barely furnished:

The mattresses and box springs on the beige
carpeted floor and roaches perched in secret

in the corners of the kitchen. The long gray
cabinets—in them just enough formula

for the week—. The mirrored coffee table
bordered in brass and cluttered with loose

change, Blue Magic, and a wide-toothed comb.
The ficus in the corner of the living room—

the way dust collected on its leaves made
the appendages look like cleft geodes in light.

The year is 1985 and the mother's grandmother
is still alive. No one she loves yet has contracted

HIV or has died by heart attack or overdose—.
My mother when she was young, her jade

hair permed and pressed into a bob, red lipstick
finished around the curves of her lips—.

I can imagine her when she was young
before—
                    before—
                                        before—

THE NIGHT IS AN ERUPTION OF NEBULAS

A pipe is a globe of loss—the baby

        has no diapers   and auntie had to bring some by.

Women on the street scream   and yell at

      motherfuckers.   The men snore and groan

on the curbside. You empty your pockets—

      bobby pins   and dimes   and lint—

on the dresser. The mirror   with the baby's finger-

      prints on it.   The lights aren't back on yet—

but the baby's   father comes back.

      You make love by candlelight.

The woman from upstairs says *I fucked your man*

      in your car. Finally, you get the courage

to leave.   Eviction comes first. Credit score

      plummets like an airplane.   You make the baby

a pool for her dolls with a ceramic bowl.

      Your mother says you can come home   for a while.

You make $4.25 an hour as a bank teller. The baby's father

      puts a red bow in her hair before you pick her up—.

He has always made you smile.

      The night is an eruption of nebulas—

you pat the baby's back to get her to sleep.   *Shhh.*

      Casual sirens fade.   She is your reason for being

until a man touches you.   You call back the married man

      you think is the love of your life.   He says *Baby*

on the answering machine. You make another life

      together in the only tenderness you know—

then you make that life disappear   without a name.

      You killed my son—the love of your life says.

You think,   *Men will never know what it is to carry*
   a life   *when you can't even burden your own.*

Husband Home from the Marines

She grabs orange juice for her eldest—
    oatmeal for the morning, garlic

and red onion to simmer the beans in
    for dinner. Her husband was not there

when she came home from work, and this
    baby she carries always craves

shortbread. The woman at the counter
    asks—*When are you due?*

October, she replies. Her husband
    of six months seems to have finally

found a job he'll stay on for more than
    a month. He is different now

that he's come home from the desert—
    grinds his teeth at night—not the boy

she knew who called her Kimmy
    and wore dress shoes and ties

every day. She avoids telling him
    she's seen the stash of whiskey

he keeps in his coat next to his Marlboros
    or that his father called, said *Yes*,

he can help pay the rent this month.
    It's a ten-minute drive home.

Mother and daughter laugh as they carry
　　　the groceries into the apartment.

My father yells—*Where have you been?*
　　　My mother says, *Down the street at*

Lucky's. Tim, please, I don't want to start.
　　　She grips tighter the plastic bags,

the fibers begin to thin with weight.
　　　The eldest child runs into the living

room, resumes playing dolls on the floor. *No*
　　　pregnant woman should be out this late.

I bet that baby isn't even mine.
　　　The beatings won't start until after

she gives birth and he says, *The baby*
　　　doesn't look like my family.

She holds her tongue. No need to start
　　　his fists early.

FAMILY LORE

For Tanecia and Kenia

The apartment complex was made to mirror a park.
The greenery and open space made it seem the earth
was our own. My mother worked in Saratoga—
in an office with white people, and we could afford
to live. Our neighbors stole the bunny we kept in a cage
on the back porch and would leave the swimming
pool each time we used our key to enter through
the gate. We didn't care, our music, our laughter—
something we had earned by then. We lived there
before I was old enough to be beaten, before the divorce—
my father's mind not yet completely broken. In that home,
my cousin and sister taught me to say the words *apple*
and *banana*. Until I was two, I would babble *banana*
when I meant *apple* and *apple* when I meant *banana*—
a cute quirk, an inverse, of a baby's tongue.
What matters is that they fed me. My sister taught me
the sidewalk was a runway. She practiced her walk
outside the apartment by the needlegrass,
the pentameter of her bounce ascending almost
as high as the medallion foothills in the background.
She walked forward with her shoulders back as if
she were a woman emerging from a fire without regret.
My cousin cheered her on, said to me *Boo Boo, that's how
you do it*—walk like a supermodel. What matters is that
they held me. I was their baby, just a year old, and
they made sure I was always with them, teaching me
everything they knew. When they were done pretending,

they helped each other lift me onto their bike—with all
of their eight-year-old might. I was on the handlebars,
my sister intended to pedal, and my cousin hopped on
the pegs as the wheels began to spin. The wheels never
finished a full rotation and I fell before movement became
a swift gesture loss. Isn't it like this when we try to carry
the ones we love? You want to take them with you—
even when you cannot sustain yourself. Our story tells me
something of endings: *The world will try to take everything you love—
hold, make taut your child arms—try with all your might to keep it.*

FUNERAL

c. SUNNYVALE, 2001

The men wiped sweat
from their bald heads

and the women coursed
in black hats
into the mouth of grief.

The sanctuary was full of things
I knew nothing about:

a vial of anointing oil
an amethyst sweat cloth

slung over the sharp bishop's suit
a twisted cross hung

high on the wall, a portrait
of a white man—his eyes
pale and unmoved.

My father, Uncle Koot, and
Uncle Larry pulled at their mother
the way children do—

>   *Come on, Mama*
>   *Come on, Mama*

—trying to coax her down
from her daughter's casket.

I stood behind my grandmother
knee deep the anguish
of not knowing

where the person goes
when she detaches from
her body.

I chewed the word *died*
like neckbone meat

and remembered how I lay
in the grass on my back
when my mother whispered

    —*Kat died*
      —*Complications*
    —*Lupus*

—how I ran from an evening
that burned like a wick
and hid from god in a closet.

IN SAN JOSÉ, WE SLICED TOMATOES

For Nana

Behind your mobile home, we tended
weeds and a narrow patch of soil—just
enough for tomato bushes to grow along
wire cages in slight ribbons of sunlight.
In the kitchen, you held the knife, said,
This is what my mama used to do, then
reached into a ceramic bowl of salt, swirled
your hand almost like god dusting sour
crystals over the fruit. You said, *We used to
grow our own food and catch jackrabbits
with sling shots and rocks in the wood.*
I was only a child when you gave me this
story and knew little of the way of the past.
I sat on my knees listening at the kitchen
table and imagined you and your eight
siblings—running through the deep green
Aiken woods, the jackrabbit—his long limbs
in a slow crawl, his fawn ears elongated
for fear of being caught. Heard your siblings
whisper—*Elsie! Get in position!* I imagined
your small hands carrying the carcass
to your mother. How pleased you must have
been to have provided good meat—the same
as you were when you placed that fat, fleshy,
and halved tomato in my hand remembering.
You were right—*Home is where the heart is
broken and buried.* Now as I think of you then,
mouth full of tomatoes and story, I retrace
the vermillion steps of my memory, wonder
why we let each other go. I want the past to
tell me something different of our ending—
History tells me this is too much to ask.

ELEGY

For Julius Upson

What I remember is the morning brightly pouring in
through the glass in the front door.

The school bus only a few minutes away, and you
taking the time.

My sister had taught me to grab the shoestrings
by the ears like a bunny pulled from a hat

but it never worked.

We sat on the floor in the living room
Mema never allowed us to sit in—

    Loop then swoop then pull—.

Your motions slow enough for me to follow.
    You clapped when I got it—

Paw-Paw is proud of you. I think

of those small moments now almost eleven years
after your burial and wish I had the courage then
to say what I can now:

You were my only

source of gentleness: the way you danced
    with my grandmother around the garage
to Aretha, calling her *Cakes*. Drank pop
    with the grandkids as we all pretended
we were grown and drunk.

The way you called my mother, your stepchild,

Daughter.

How could I have known then we would end so soon?
As I climbed onto the bus with my shoes tied,

you watched as I rode away—my brother at your side
in a diaper and white socks. The sun just beginning

to careen over the Sierras as you waved goodbye

with a cowboy hat on your head, a Budweiser
in your hands, and a cigarette in your mouth

just beginning to burn—.

Even Now—

My mother pushes
    these memories around

with her tongue. Hesitates
    then tells me about the way

you jaunted in your wheelchair—
    one hand over an opened

Bible and a secret pistol
    cocked and hidden

beneath a quilt shawling
    your residual limbs—

while the other hand reached
    over a pot of greens.

All these years later, my mother
    still says—*Big Mama*

nursed my father, her youngest,
    after he drank himself into

psychosis. Even now, loneliness
    is a portal I enter.

There I meet you both—
    wheelchair and wheelchair,

Jimmy's drooping face,
   and your hands brushing

his greying wool hair.
   My mother manages

only cool whispers of her
   past, summoning from

the earth each of your molecules,
   summoning from me

tendon and heartbone.

Forgiveness Pantoum

c. Tyler, Texas, 2018

All stories about my grandfather refuse to end:
I loved him and I have tried hard to forgive him.
My mother says this to my uncle. *Remember?*
Dad would drive us drunk up the mountain.

We loved him, and we tried hard to forgive him.
She stops herself before she mentions the tang
of gin on his breath. *We were terrified, remember,*
as he drove us to Half Moon Bay. She pauses

perhaps, recalling an open blue sky or the tang
of fear on her siblings' Black faces and how beautiful
green cliffs could be, even that close to falling. Pausing
she never mentions the ocean, only the winding

Pontiac suffering up the mountain's brink, beautiful
with memory. *Jimmy was hard to love, but I forgave him.*
In memory, my mother cradles her father winding
in a long black ache, burdening that man to her end.

In the Opposite Direction of Home, the Road

signed *Yosemite National Park 85 miles,* curves
and splits a field of alfalfa. Heat breaches
from the sun's corona bearing down directly
above this agrarian section of earth. The Sierra
Nevada is not as clear as I remembered them—
granite monoliths of the planet's evolution stalking
a bright and clear sky. Now only the mountain's
yellow base is visible in the smog. In my rearview
mirror, a man works a field alone along the feet
of this mountain. For a moment, I do not notice
my foot off the gas—60 miles per hour slowing
to nothing but a mess of color and motion
and the erupting shimmer glosses the hot tar
surface of the county road. The man reminds me
of another man hardened in the memory
of my grandmother—her father. Daddy Buster,
the sharecropper who labored until his hands were
black with toil, calloused with the need to feed a wife
and fifteen children. Once, I asked my grandmother
for his story, and she said, *No, we can't dwell on the past.
Know we didn't suffer too much. God will turn us to salt
if we look back at everything we've lost or never had.*

Our Past Bowed Like the Branches of a Madrone Tree

I have taken with me what is left: your pajama pants
   Pawpaw's green flannel robe,   the worn leather   belts creased
by your hands.
     I have scavenged
       the photo albums,   filed the pictures   in this archive.
        Let them dry
           like Nootka roses between pages,
                  wanting them
to leave me with stains of magenta.   Imperfectly kept,   pressed
     between my longing.   There is no name   for our grief—
           just its music
the way its melody leaves   the mouth—
        demanding the body
                buckle.

In late summer,
     I sat sweating in your living
           room, flipped through photos
of us,   counted our dead. Our past selves
        bound within the confines of light
marked and shuttered   against time,
           trying
            to find ourselves
within   the promise of
        future. In the west,
   the sun lifts herself
        over the Sierra Nevada
   and closes   on the ocean,   shutting us in at the end
of her book.   A bandit of light,

           a halo shown   around the wound—

                                  the source

of so much fluorescent   pain. What else should we call this

                          song of memory?

       The history of ourselves

              fettered in some secret,

                     uninhabitable place.

EPILOGUE

If I write this, everything about us will be true—
                the turned-over tables—
        the bat you threatened my brother with—
        the knife he threatened me with—the time
                I punched his asthmatic chest
        wishing he would die; within
                truth, there can be no metaphors
for violence or love or violence
        committed in the act of love; time
is the enemy—our former selves
        tacked to its walls, battered,
                tender and sorry
        for all the ways we were wrong;
                        I was wrong—
caught in an endless negotiation
        with the past, with every possibility
of escape lost by loving you
                despite;
        Mother, I am in a perpetual state of falling—
                I am trying
                        to make you an archive,
latch onto the stories of our bodies—
        a long blanket of stars—
                tell; every truth bound
in subtle balm and in a subtle leverage
        of pain; we might not survive the span
                of my need to say this—

Births and Deaths: A Chronology

1814:   Mary Ellen "Mammy" Pleasant born enslaved in Georgia.

1850:   California Slave Law is enacted.

1858:   Mary Ellen Pleasant hides fugitive slave boy (Archy) in her home until she can find him passage from San Francisco to Canada.

1904:   Mary Ellen Pleasant dies penniless in San Francisco.

190(?):   Marie Gage born in Mississippi.

1907:   Lonnie "Buster" Ross born in Texas.

1909:   Cedaliah Harris born to a white mother (who abandons her) and Negro father who raises her in Texas.

1911:   James Lee Eiland born in Mississippi.

1929:   Joseph "Joe" Hughes born in Chattanooga, Tennessee.

193(?):   Cedaliah Harris and Lonnie Ross marry.

Buster is a sharecropper and is the only Negro in Overton County, Texas, who knows how to work a plough machine. They raise a family in a three-room house a mile from their church.

Marie Gage and James Lee Eiland marry.

1933:   Jimmy born in Noxapater, Mississippi, to James Lee and Marie.

1935:   Elsie Twigg born in Aiken, South Carolina.

1942–1945:   More than 50,000 African Americans migrate to the East Bay.

1944:   Myra (eighth of fifteen children) born to Cedaliah and Buster in Overton, Texas.

195(?):   Jimmy enlists in Korean War.

Myra's older brother—"Punk"—enlists in Korean War.

Myra's older siblings move to the San Francisco Bay Area.

1955:   Jimmy, his brothers, his mother (Marie) move to Redwood City, California.

195(?):   Joe and Elsie marry.

1959:   Myra graduates from high school and follows her siblings to Redwood City.

1960:	Jimmy and Myra marry.
1962:	Tim born in Aiken, South Carolina, to Elsie and Joe.
	Joe and Elsie move their family from Aiken to Redwood City so that Joe can start a trucking business.
	Rodney born to Jimmy and Myra in San Mateo, California.
1963:	Kim born to Jimmy and Myra in San Mateo.
1965:	Watts Riots erupt in the Watts neighborhood and surrounding areas in Los Angeles.
1966:	Jimmy and Myra's third child (Tammy) born in San Mateo.
	Black Panther Party founded in Oakland, California, by Huey P. Newton and Bobby Seale.
1969:	Fred Hampton Sr. is assassinated in his home in Chicago— sleeping next to his partner and child.
1970:	James III "Boo" born to Jimmy and Myra in San Mateo.
	East Palo Alto is in violation of desegregation laws.
1975:	James Lee dies.
197(?):	Jimmy and Myra divorce.
1977:	Buster dies.
1980:	Myra marries Julius Upson.
	They move from East Palo Alto to San José.
	At fourteen years old, Kim moves in with Marie "Big Mama" Gage in her Redwood City apartment.
1981:	Crack cocaine is invented.
	HIV/AIDS epidemic begins.
1983:	East Palo Alto is incorporated as a city.
1984:	Ronald Reagan signs the Comprehensive Crime Control Act of 1984.
1985:	Tanecia is born to Kim in Redwood City.
1988:	Tim enlists in the Marines.
1989:	Huey P. Newton dies.
1991:	Marie Gage dies.
	Latasha Harlins is murdered.

Kim marries Tim after he comes home from the Marines.

1992: LA Riots follow after a jury acquits four police officers of police brutality against Rodney King.

Erica born to Kim and Tim in Redwood City.

Joseph Hughes dies.

1993: Myra and Julius buy an acre of farmland in the San Joaquin Valley.

1994: Jared born to Kim and Tim in Redwood City.

Bill Clinton signs the Violent Crime Control and Law Enforcement Act of 1994.

1996: Kim files for divorce.

2001: Twin Towers burn.

2004: Jimmy dies.

Facebook moves to Palo Alto.

2006: Cedaliah Ross dies.

2008: Housing market crashes.

2010: Julius dies.

2013: Erica leaves California for the first time.

Notes

Book epigraph is from Saidiya Hartman, *Lose Your Mother: A Journey Along the Atlantic Slave Route* (Macmillan, 2008).

"Triptych" epigraph is from Audre Lorde's poem "Outside" in *The Collected Poems of Audre Lorde* (W. W. Norton, 2000).

"Rupture in Memory" takes a line from Louise Glück's poem "Faithful and Virtuous Night" in *Faithful and Virtuous Night* (Farrar, Straus and Giroux, 2014).

First epigraph for Part 2 is from Christina Sharpe, *In the Wake: On Blackness and Being* (Duke University Press, 2016).

Second epigraph for Part 2 is from Delilah L. Beasley, *The Negro Trailblazers of California* (Book Jungle, 2007).

Epigraph for Part 3 is from Natasha Trethewey's poem "Letters from Storyville" in *Bellocq's Ophelia: Poems* (Graywolf Press, 2002).

"Bois Caïman" is a voodoo ceremony performed by enslaved Africans in Haiti before the beginning of their revolt against their French enslavers.

Toussaint Louverture (1743–1803) was a Haitian general, former governor-general of Saint-Domingue, and revolutionary leader during the Haitian Revolution, which began in 1791.

ACKNOWLEDGMENTS

These poems have appeared, sometimes in different versions, in the following magazines:

BOAAT Journal ("I Called Home in January")

Poet Lore ("In San José, We Sliced Tomatoes")

The Offing ("Rippling Through the Dark")

wildness magazine ("My Mother at Twenty-One")

Hot Metal Bridge ("Funeral")

Chicago Quarterly Review ("Our Past Bowed Like the Branches of a Madrone Tree," "Beckwourth Pass," "Meet-Cute in San Mateo County," and "The Way We Were")

Passages North (from "The Accounts of Mammy Pleasant" section 11)

Guernica ("The Night is an Eruption of Nebulas")

RHINO Poetry ("Portrait of My Father)

Jazz and Culture Journal ("Black Women Standing Ankle-Deep in Pacific Water," "In the Opposite Direction of Home, the Road," and "Routine").

Also, I would like to thank E. Ethelbert Miller, my first mentor in poetry, who welcomed me with kindness and generosity and taught me to *trust* the uniqueness of my own voice. Your generosity changed my life.

Lastly, I would like to thank my friends—who read and reread each of these poems. Your love sustains me.

ABOUT THE AUTHOR

E. Hughes's poems have been published or are forthcoming in *The Rumpus*, *Guernica Magazine*, *Poet Lore*, *Indiana Review*, and *Gulf Coast Magazine*— among other outlets. They are a Cave Canem fellow and have been a finalist for the 2021 Elinor Benedict Poetry Prize, longlisted for the 2021 Granum Fellowship Prize, and a semifinalist of the 2022 and 2023 92Y Discovery Contest. In 2021, they received their MFA+MA from the Litowitz Creative Writing Program at Northwestern University. Currently, Hughes is a PhD student in philosophy at Emory University, studying black aesthetics, psychoanalysis, and poststructuralism.

ABOUT HAYMARKET BOOKS

Haymarket Books is a radical, independent, nonprofit book publisher based in Chicago. Our mission is to publish books that contribute to struggles for social and economic justice. We strive to make our books a vibrant and organic part of social movements and the education and development of a critical, engaged, and internationalist Left.

We take inspiration and courage from our namesakes, the Haymarket Martyrs, who gave their lives fighting for a better world. Their 1886 struggle for the eight-hour day—which gave us May Day, the international workers' holiday—reminds workers around the world that ordinary people can organize and struggle for their own liberation. These struggles—against oppression, exploitation, environmental devastation, and war—continue today across the globe.

Since our founding in 2001, Haymarket has published more than nine hundred titles. Radically independent, we seek to drive a wedge into the risk-averse world of corporate book publishing. Our authors include Angela Y. Davis, Arundhati Roy, Keeanga-Yamahtta Taylor, Eve L. Ewing, aja monet, Mariame Kaba, Naomi Klein, Rebecca Solnit, Mohammed El-Kurd, José Olivarez, Noam Chomsky, Winona LaDuke, Robyn Maynard, Leanne Betasamosake Simpson, Howard Zinn, Mike Davis, Marc Lamont Hill, Dave Zirin, Astra Taylor, and Amy Goodman, among many other leading writers of our time. We are also the trade publishers of the acclaimed Historical Materialism Book Series.

Haymarket also manages a vibrant community organizing and event space in Chicago, Haymarket House, the popular Haymarket Books Live event series and podcast, and the annual Socialism Conference.

Also Available from Haymarket Books

All the Blood Involved in Love, Maya Marshall

Black Queer Hoe, Britteney Black Rose Kapri

The BreakBeat Poets Vol. 2: Black Girl Magic, edited by
  Mahogany L. Browne, Idrissa Simmonds, and Jamila Woods

Build Yourself a Boat, Camonghne Felix

Can I Kick It?, Idris Goodwin

Citizen Illegal, José Olivarez

I Remember Death by Its Proximity to What I Love,
  Mahogany L. Browne

Lineage of Rain, Janel Pineda

A Map of My Want, Faylita Hicks

Milagro, Penelope Allegria

Nazar Boy, Tarik Dobbs

O Body, Dan "Sully" Sullivan

The Patron Saint of Making Curfew, Tim Stafford

Rifqa, Mohammed El-Kurd

Super Sad Black Girl, Diamond Sharp

There Are Trans People Here, H. Melt

Too Much Midnight, Krista Franklin